Paint Your Way to the American Dream!

Paint Your Way to the American Dream!

*Create a Business Empire With the
Stroke of Your Paint Brush!*

Kurt Degen

To order additional copies of this book, contact:
Xlibris
844-714-8691
www.Xlibris.com
Orders@Xlibris.com
849842

CONTENTS

I dedicate this book to my wife, family and friends for all their love and support through out the years.

Introduction

In many ways, the story I'm about to tell you isn't unique. There have always been ordinary people like myself, building successful businesses, taking what they have and turning it into something special. I wanted to share my story because I truly believe that with the right attitude and plenty of hard work, anyone can get out there and make money. There is no secret to it, only perseverance, pragmatism and that special element - really phenomenal customer service. I want to share with you in this short book everything I've learned being in the painting business for over three decades now. If you are looking to start your own painting business, or if you have a business that you are trying to grow, this book can help you. Even if you're trying to make money in some other industry, I believe these principles are the key to developing your skill and reputation as an entrepreneur who delivers real value to his clients.

My Story

It all started after I left Plymouth State College. I came down to Miami, Florida, still a kid, stars in my eyes and honestly really excited about starting my life. I ended up working for a large newspaper company for a year and a half. I was just 21 years old at the time, and when you're that young, any experience is good experience - you're just glad to have a job. If you know anything about me, you'll know that I'm a pretty energetic person, and that I like to move and keep things going. Sure, office work got a little stale at times, but these were just the sacrifices you made as an adult, right?

I learned a lot, but after I had the opportunity to grow a little, I started to get the sinking impression that it just wasn't going anywhere. I would show up day after day and do my thing, but I always felt trapped there, quietly making money for someone else. Just a year and a half into my adult working life, I knew that corporate America was not for me.

You could say I've always had a restless spirit, and eventually I left the newspaper company and started doing a few odd jobs. To this day I wonder what would have happened if I had lacked the guts and had decided that leaving was too risky.

Would I be like those older employees, inching slowly towards their retirements, tired to their bones and completely uninspired with their work and their lives? I made the decision that even if I didn't know exactly what I was going to do yet, I knew that I *wasn't* going to end up like that. My father was a successful businessman, so I was fortunate to have a good role model close at hand. Once I knew that there was so much more out there beyond the four walls of the office, I couldn't take my work as seriously anymore. Call it luck, call it youthful arrogance, but my corporate career eventually came to an end, and my new career began.

A group that renovated rentals into condominiums offered to pay me 5 dollars an hour to help with painting. They would convert these old places into condos and needed a casual contractor to do the painting. I was a young, able kid and happy to do it. I needed the money, but more importantly, there was something refreshing about painting after doing so much dull office work. Something about turning up for work and doing the best I could with the paint and rollers, something about the satisfaction of a good, hard day's work was just what I needed.

The paint was all one color to keep the condos uniform, but after a while, a few people approached me and started to ask if I could paint their condos a different color. I said yes.

Looking back, that was the first small turning point for me, the first step in a journey that would teach me more than I could have ever imagined. I felt a little thrill at being completely independent and able to work on my own terms. It was exciting. I met with them, gave them an estimate for the job, and almost immediately, I went from $5 to $40 an hour. I learned quickly that by doing nothing other than working for yourself and not others, your hourly rate could be almost ten times more. I started to get ideas.

By getting out there and really talking to people, I found that the work was plentiful. Word traveled in the condo establishments and more people approached me. They liked my work. I kept up as best as I could by learning about the trade at every opportunity. Back then, I didn't know much about painting, so the learning curve was steep. I had to quickly pick up the lingo, figure out how I was going to charge these people, where I would get my supplies, all of it. I knew nothing about the kinds of paint, the tools, how to calculate areas - I basically winged it for those first few contracts. I'm grateful for those condo days because I learned early on that really taking care of your customers was the key to growth. *I wasn't entirely sure what I was doing, but I knew that when I kept my customers happy, it all worked out!*

By the time the condo work ran out, the entrepreneurial bug had bitten me. I didn't know it yet, but I was already getting a strong sense of the direction I wanted to take in life. What I liked best was not so much the painting, but that I was entirely independent. It was me, the customer and the work. No complicated hierarchies, no crushing sense of boredom, no meetings, nothing. At that point, I could have tried to squash myself back into the corporate role and find another "proper job" but I was curious and enjoying myself too much. I realized that I had had nothing to be afraid of.

I kept things fluid, curious to see where the work would take me. I started to dabble with carpet cleaning and cleaning services to boost the painting work, but I always came back to the painting. The whole process was very organic, but slowly I started roping in referrals. The people at the condo liked the work and referred me to their friends, and they referred me to *their* friends. I saw firsthand that a satisfied customer could earn you five more referrals down the line. While I learned how to paint properly, where to find equipment and all the rest, I was also learning how to interact with our customers, finding exactly how to keep them satisfied. I never turned anyone down. I just wanted to grasp whatever I could and when someone expressed interest, I jumped at the chance. I have been doing that with customers ever since. *I still try to remember to treat them as though they were as precious to me as those first few clients. Because, well, they are!*

At that point, I had a steady flow of around five referrals a day and almost all of that stemmed from the original people we painted for in the condos. The condo business was very lucrative, and I was perfectly set to take advantage of it. My company's reputation slowly grew, even though I did almost no advertising back then. Every new customer came from another satisfied customer, the customers were the lifeline, the customers *were* the business. Eventually, I put more effort into advertising, what kept things rolling over was that the customers were satisfied, and came back for repeat business.

Soon, the days with Corporate America became a distant memory and I couldn't believe, that I stayed there for as long as I did. I did not like the idea of being owned by a corporate body, working hard and earning money for other people. In a year and a half with Corporate America, nothing much had changed but after just a few months of doing painting, things were developing, things were getting exciting. I'm not going to say that everything just fell into place easily. In the beginning, it was difficult and a lot of the time, I didn't quite know what I was doing. But there was one constant in all the changes my company went through: excellent customer service. As long as I kept my eye on the client, I had a growing stream of referrals. It all rested on the excellent service my company provided.

What I was building in the early days was my own sense of freedom. It was exhilarating, I did not answer to anyone, I became more confident. I learned that if I was going to succeed, it was up to me and me only. What started out as a small dream, became lucrative and successful. When I think of how little I started with, I can't believe how far I came. Just a few rollers, some paint and a contact here and there became a thriving company that offered something of real value to its customers.

In many ways, I think that if I wasn't in such a tight spot to begin with, I wouldn't have worked so hard and been as successful. I see what happens to young entrepreneurs today, who have some disposable income: they have their plans, but having a safety net actually makes them take *fewer* risks and not work as hard. When I was starting out, all I had was about $100 and a car. There was no time to think about things, to doubt myself, to get caught up in business plans. I had to make it work, end of story. I bought some paint, a few rollers and I went out there. At the forefront of my mind was turning that $100 into more, so I *had* to do good work, to wow my customers. If I wanted to make money, I had no choice!

When you're in dire straits like I was, when you know that the quality of your work and your entire business is resting on you coming up with something good and quickly, you will find a way. Your brain starts to look for solutions, you're energized to do good work, and you're *hungry*. That's how I turned that $100 into something more.

Part of the appeal of being an entrepreneur is the satisfaction you get from working for yourself, being accountable to nobody else but yourself. As time went on and I continued to get more work, I had to hire on more workers. But to grow, I would need to be responsible for my workers, to make sure that I always had payroll covered. Growth can be scary, but you need to do it.

As the business expanded, I understood that if I wanted the big jobs, we'd have to change and adapt. The business had started officially in around 1982, and by about 1989, I was managing approximately, $80,000 - $90,000 annually. Even though it was more than I could have dreamed of as a kid a few years prior, I knew that it was just the beginning. Some people had moved on, but with others I had started to develop good and lasting relationships.

When you see these businessmen who've made millions, you don't see all the work that went into it, you just see the end result. You think to yourself, maybe they were lucky, or maybe they have some special business skills that the rest of us don't. Have you ever read these business biographies? It can be intimidating. You think, fine, that's all well and good, but *I* could never do that.

But the truth is, there's no secret to it at all. It's just hard work, turning up on time and treating your clients properly. The funny thing is, I was not *that* good a painter but with time and hard work, I got better and better. I realize how important it is to do a good job, to be clean, to be conscientious about the people's homes you're going into, to be on time, to turn up to the job with a smile. Follow protocol. Take pride in your work. Painting is just painting, but when you offer a complete experience, when you offer people painting that is clean and professional and you do a job that makes them feel taken care of, it's more than just painting.

It might be a funny thing to say, but this whole country needs to be painted, and I'm serious about that. It's ridiculous. It's something people never think about, but your house, your office, your industrial buildings, your condos - that all needs painting, sometimes, pretty regularly. If you want to make money in this industry, you can make money. If you want to be filthy rich, you can be filthy rich. If you're willing to work hard, the work is there.

Today, I am comfortably retired and would like to share my experience and success with anyone wanting to start a successful painting business.

Chapter One

LET'S GET STARTED!

Building something out of nothing can be really intimidating! It's only natural to have lots of questions, so here I'll answer some of the most common ones.

Q: Why should I start a <u>Painting</u> <u>Business?</u>

Like I said, I got into painting almost by accident. I enjoyed the work and if you do too, that's a good enough reason. But another reason is that, compared to some other similar businesses, it's pretty easy to get started. Paint work is also something that almost everyone needs, and they will need it again and again as time goes on.

And most importantly, if you do a good job, word of mouth spreads quickly. As I'll discuss below, painting is a business about referrals. If you want to start a business that rewards you for your good work and going the extra mile to please your customers, this could be the business for you.

Q: How do I get good at painting?

Honestly, I learned to get good at painting on the job when I started. I started out painting walls and quickly figured out how to be neat and conscientious. You'll be surprised how you get better and faster at painting with a little bit of practice.

One idea would be to work for a larger painting company and get the experience you need then go out on your own after learning the tricks of the trade and are more comfortable with the actual art of painting. Just remember practice makes perfect and sometimes you just have to jump in and get your feet wet and learn each day.

If you're totally at a loss, go to work for an existing paint company for a couple weeks or a month. You'll get a feel for how it works and if you like the way they do things, follow their procedure.

Q: What equipment do I need, and how do I get it?

When I started out, all I had were brushes, rollers, and a five-gallon bucket, all available at your local paint store. If you really have no money at all to get started, borrow $50 from a friend for seed money, or you could do odd jobs. The ideas are endless.

As time goes on and you want to grow, you'll want to get more equipment, which I will discuss in Part Two.

Q: What About The Paint?

I would highly recommend that your first step in beginning your painting business, would be to get yourself a representative at one of the more popular painting companies. I have had the same rep for the past 30 years. It is important early on to establish yourself with a paint store. Paint stores give special prices to contractors, so shop around for the best deal and then sign a contract with the store of your choice.

That way, you will be able to please the customer who is buying the paint by getting them your discounted price, which makes everyone happy. I also signed on as a member with the PDCA (*The Painting and Decorating Contractors of America*). They were very helpful in guiding me at the early stages of my business. You can get their contact information online.

If you are really strapped for cash, you can have the customer buy the paint as an advance cost. If you do this, factor it into the price you'll charge for the work. I found that a lot of customers liked to do this so they could pick out the paint and know exactly what they were getting.

Having said that, always have a suggestion of your own for the quality of the paint – the customer will value your opinion and expertise. Customers almost always have lots of questions and you should be prepared to answer them.

Some of the most common questions were what type of paint should they use?

Do I use a different paint on the exterior of my house than on the interior. What brand of paint is best were the two most common questions asked.

First of all, every Paint and Home Improvement store carry their own particular brand and quality level.

It is very important to know what type of paint to use inside versus the exterior of the house. There are basically four types of paints that I work with. Flat (matte) eggshell, satin and semi gloss. A satin paint is what I use on the exterior of the house. It has a seal that keeps the paint from fading, is more weather resistant and easier to pressure clean out any collected dirt than a matte paint would be. For the inside you may want to use an eggshell or matte finish paint depending on the preference of the client.

Q: How do I get my first jobs?

I was lucky enough to get my first jobs from working in the condo development, but there are a lot of ways to put yourself out there and find work.

When you're just starting out, you probably won't get much work from wandering around knocking on doors, but you can offer to work for people who know you: referrals from friends, relatives, neighbors, etc. You can take an ad out in the local paper, home magazines, hand out flyers, business cards, use Home Improvement websites and social media.

The paint store where you buy your paint will allow you to put flyers up. Grocery stores may or may not, but the worst that can happen is they take them down.

Q: How do I turn a little jobs into a lot of jobs?

Two ways: advertising and referrals. Let's take those one at a time.

Working Is Advertising

We've just talked about how to advertise to get your first job. But remember, as you are working, you are also advertising. Put a sign for your company on your truck or your van. If you can't do that, put a sign on the lawn of the house as you're working.

Painting the outside of a house is better advertisement than painting the inside. When you start painting the outside, you get a ton of exposure. Neighbors see you out there and if you are working in a nice manner, they may stop and ask for your information.

Referrals Are Your Lifeblood

But in my experience, referrals are the most important part of the business. Here's what you should know to get good referrals:

★ Don't be afraid to actually ask for a referral from your satisfied customers. Let people know that as part of your efforts to be the best at what you do, you rely on word-of-mouth referrals. Frame this as a way they can show their appreciation for excellent work you do. You could put "referrals appreciated" on your business card or quote, or you could just drop it into conversation.

★ First impressions count but don't forget about last impressions. Leave them with something to remember you by after the job is completed. I've seen people give away promotional items - fridge magnets, calendars, a little discount or some other little things. It's nice, and it keeps you on their minds.

★ Make referring people easy and obvious. Don't leave your client guessing about the best way to get a hold of you and refer someone else. Tell them what the process is and make it quick and easy. Have a few channels open: email, phone, social networks etc.

★ Don't forget to say thank you. After the job is done, send a note or make a call, and if it's appropriate, ask for feedback. Really give them the impression that you are grateful for their business and are happy to have it. You can get someone to organize an automated letter or hire someone to write them regularly if you need to do it often enough.

★ If you have a website or LinkedIn profile, you could ask people for testimonials or a recommendation. Even people who can't think of anyone to refer will usually be happy to do this, and when you specifically ask for an opinion that will be made public, you'll be surprised how generous people can be with their feedback.

★ Referrals come from your paint store too. This is yet another reason to maintain a good relationship with them, because they can provide you with leads on more business.

★ Don't just take! Make a habit of referring people to other businesses who have related clientele and you may win a referral when they are busy or approached by someone they can't help. As they say, the best way to get a referral is to make a referral!

Q: How do I know what to charge?

When I started out, I made a lot of mistakes with pricing. I was new and so when I was not sure, I priced my services below the competition. However, if you want to make a profit and eventually grow your business, you'll need to stay on top of your costs, overheads and ultimately your profit margin. Your entire profit rests on you being able to charge accurately for your labor and material, so if you're constantly asking for nothing more than your prime costs, you're going to be going in circles for a long time. Make sure that your estimate is priced accordingly.

If you're at a loss, there's nothing wrong with doing a little market research. When I first started out, I would ask around to see what other paint companies were charging. I talked to paint stores, and even asked other painters what they would charge me for a particular job if I were the customer and it was my house. I would give the estimate, a little under the competition. In time, though, you'll get a better understanding of what your work is really worth.

Work out what profit you need at a minimum and go from there. You'll most likely give medium sized contracts lump sum estimates and you'll likely be paying $15 to $25 per hour for your workers. These are fixed, so you'll need to work around them. Do this quick exercise for a given job. Take the total sales and deduct the cost of your materials. Include in that figure your overhead, your tools, everything that you will need to complete the job. Now divide that amount by the number of hours you worked on that job to get the per hour value that you made. Is it acceptable? Is it actually higher than what you've been going with so far? If so, you may be setting yourself up for debt and maybe worse.

Now, before you're tempted to say that if you price yourself too high, you won't attract customers. Try to think through possible solutions. When you establish yourself as a reputable, trustworthy company, people are going to be OK with paying more. If you go with paints that are pricier than the usual, try to sell the product to clients in terms of quality. Play up their environmental friendliness, the depth of color, the durability, how long the paint job will last with better paint quality. You're not just justifying the expense, you're establishing yourself in their eyes as someone who cares about quality, and this will make them trust you and be more willing to pay what it actually costs to do a good paint job.

Measure Properly

To make sure that you have an ample enough profit margin, you're going to need to fine-tune your method of measuring the surface you intend to paint. Don't guess or estimate. Draw up a worksheet for every job. Make note of the square meters or feet, the surface you're painting, include labor and the materials you'll be using and add any tools you'll need to complete the job. A lot of times you have to add on for baseboards. You have to add on for doors because people will probably want everything done, although sometimes they don't. You also have to take into consideration the furniture because the furniture could take as long to move around, and then get around, as actually painting the room.

Managing costs gets more complicated when you have workers. At K&T, we made our own "work order form" that simplified our lives a great deal. On it, we had painters note down the start and end time of the project, the number of rooms, what work was being done (for example painting, touching up, sanding, fixing drywall etc.) as well as the worker's name and how many hours they worked, plus special instructions and the client's final authorization. You could also make room for details of the surface, the total area etc., depending on whether you charge per hour or per job.

Name of Company   *WORK ORDER FORM*

Job Site: _____

Name of Contact and Phone #: _____

Day/Date: _____ **Time In**_____ **Out**_____

Work Done: Patch ( ) Sand ( ) Prime ( ) Paint ( ) Caulk ( ) Epoxy ( )

Description of Work

Exterior of House

Interior of House

Other Work Performed etc......

Name of Painter	Time-in	Time-out

Make sure every single one of your painters is an expert at reading and implementing the manufacturer's spread rate given on the side of the paint can. Decide together on the standard way you're going to convert these. Factor in that rough, stucco surfaces and corrugated iron take more paint. You might compile a small booklet of special spread rates, mixing tips or whatever else you can think of and give it to your painters; it'll be especially useful for the newbie and those starting out.

In time, you will also going to need to know how to work in inflation and adjust for changing paint prices. This will affect your overhead, too. I have had great success using "productivity charts" as well, where you gather data on not only the jobs and how they're being completed, but the output for each member of the staff. These are particularly helpful when you want to decide who to promote, who to give bonuses to and who could benefit from a little more training.

I'll talk more about adding workers in Part Two.

Above all, remember that people are usually willing to pay more for excellent customer service. I'll talk about that in Part Three.

Q: How do I get the most value out of every job?

Treat every job you get as a springboard into new opportunities. I have found over and over again that when you show up, there's more work to be done than what you initially discussed with the customer. You could say, "I'm just here to paint the inside like we said." Or, you could think like an entrepreneur and offer to do the extra work. I am a firm believer that no job is too small or beneath me to do.

Sometimes it's as simple as this: the customer hires you to paint the inside of the house, but you see that the outside could use some paint too, and offer to do that work. Remember, outside jobs are great advertising. They're also more lucrative – outside jobs are more straightforward than inside, because you don't have to move furniture or cover everything in cloth. Later, when you can afford a sprayer, this work will go even faster.

The customer might need some other things done. If you're handy enough to replace rotted fascia board outside, replace doors, or replace water-stained drywall, do it. There are a lot of little extra things that they'll ask you to do and if you think you can do it well, do it. That's how you can turn a $2,000 job into a $4,000 job. If you can't do it yourself, you can bring in someone you trust who can do it. Just *never* take on an aspect of the job that you can't do well, because no matter how well you paint, if you mess up another part of the job, that hurts your reputation.

My company also eventually added home improvements services. We cleaned, stained and sealed decks; we waterproofed homes; and provided refinishing and framing services. Anytime there was a new product or technique on the market, I made sure I knew about it and checked to see whether it's was something I could provide to my clients.

Did you know that interior decorators can charge hundreds of dollars an hour for advising your client on things like what colors to paint their walls? Yet, you'd be surprised how few painters know or even care about color.

You may see it as just a technical job - put the paint on the wall - but bear in mind that, especially with residential jobs, the client is probably painting the interior wall to decorate. People spend hours choosing paint colors; imagine how pleased they'd be if you stepped in and could give advice about what will look good. Do you know how natural light changes wall colors? Do you know about the color chart?

Do you know how to coordinate floor finishing's with the color you're using?

Chapter Two

GROWING YOUR BUSINESS

Someday in the not-too-distant future, if you keep doing a good job for more and more people, you'll have more work than you can do by yourself. That's when you know it's time to scale up and grow the business. But growth can be scary and presents its own challenges. This section will answer some of the most important questions about taking your business to the next level.

As you start to expand your business, it is important that you form some type of corporation, whether a LLC or "S Corp." which I had for my company. This helps you to write-off all your business expenses and it flows over to your personal taxes and allows for write-offs there as well. It also protects your personal assets in case of a lawsuit. This can be easily done on the Internet, but I recommend you go through a lawyer to compile the paper work.

Q: Where do I find Workers?

I would visit paint stores, hardware stores, home improvement stores in my area and put up Want Ads for experienced painters. I usually ended up with more responses than I needed but I always kept their names on file for the future as my business grew. Painters would also approach me for work.

Q: How do you train new Workers?

Not everyone I hired had the experience right away. I would either train them personally on the job or have my foreman train them. My best painter and most dependable worker would get promoted to a foreman. They had worked their way up by always being on time for every job, having great leadership, management and people skills with high energy and motivation.

All new workers would pair up with a more experienced worker at first until they were more comfortable with the way I operated my business. I started out working with each painter one on one until they felt confident enough and then I could send them out on their own or with another more experienced worker.

It is a good idea to make little booklets for new workers, on day to day work. Have your workers learn your system – whatever documentation you use, teach them to use it too.

It is important to train your workers from the very beginning, because they can develop bad habits if they start off the wrong way.

Q: How do you evaluate whether your workers are doing a good job?

Like I said earlier, we would keep track of everyone's productivity using a productivity chart. That's a chart that keeps track of how quickly and efficiently everyone works, and it is very useful when you're deciding who you can trust, who works hard, and who should be promoted.

Q: How does your role change when you have workers?

When you are managing your workers, you might start doing less on-site work and more coordination. You will have larger jobs, customers with more complicated needs. So, you will probably find yourself delegating responsibility to your foreman or other workers.

Just because you are not always the one holding the paintbrush, that doesn't mean you can disappear from the work sites. As the owner of your company, you need to stay visible to your customers. Have your foreman call you if the owner is going to be visiting the site, so you can come there in person. Customers want to know that you see what is going on with your crew and that you care enough to take the time to show up, even if it's just to say "hello."

Q: Do you pay your workers differently according to their ability?

Yes, I make sure all my workers were well taken care of, but the workers who have been with me the longest and do the best work made the most money. Treat them well and they will be loyal to you and do good work. I had workers stay with the company for decades.

Q: How do you land that first big job?

More often than not, your bigger jobs come from the same place as your smaller ones: referrals based on good prior work and customer service. You wouldn't believe what you can just stumble into after you've taken the time to build up your reputation. Keep doing the little jobs well and the big ones will come along.

Let me tell you a story. I was called up by a guy who was referred to me by a satisfied customer. He was a busy man and could only have the job done on a Sunday. He was renovating his kitchen and needed it painted. So, I went over and did the job myself. He was ecstatic with the results, and very pleased that I had come to do it on a Sunday.

I later found out that he was the facility manager at a huge Fortune 500 company. Two weeks later he called me and asked me to do the entire exterior of the whole facility. K&T did work for this company for over fifteen years, maintaining the relationship and giving them painting work that was as good as that first day I painted his kitchen. Without any advertising, I landed a million dollar contract with a client that gave me steady work for over fifteen years. Naturally, when other people ask me to go the extra mile for them, I'm far from put out - in fact, I see it as an opportunity to impress them and win their business for the long term. Who knows what one little favor could turn into?

I could have put him off and told him I didn't work on Sundays. I could have acted like my specific business hours were more important than satisfying my clients. But I was starting to develop a business philosophy that was about so much more than that. I was beginning to realize how important it was to offer real value to my clients, to build up on each and every experience for the long term.

Q: How do you KEEP the big jobs?

Bigger clients expect a lot from you. That's where loyalty comes in. That first big customer I got, from the man whose kitchen I painted on a Sunday, is a pharmaceutical company. They had emergency jobs that needed immediate attention, shutdowns during weekends and holidays. It was especially important to do everything they requested because the stakes were so high. I know it's not the best thing to be working over the holidays, but if you want to be an entrepreneur, and you want to make good money, and you want to keep these people happy, that's what they expect. Otherwise, they will get somebody else.

I was at their service 24/7 and was always available to them. These jobs were very profitable. Big, high stake clients put a huge premium on having people they can trust. Your track record with them is the most important thing.

Q: Once you land a big job, do you keep the smaller ones?

Smaller jobs may not be as profitable, but I held onto them for a couple reasons. The first is customer loyalty: even if I did not go out looking for small residential work anymore, I did work for the customers that I had for a long time. Second, they kept my workers busy when they were not working for my bigger clients. Steady work is important when you have workers depending on you. Plus, you can still make a few bucks for yourself while providing them with work.

Q: How do you increase your cash flow?

In order to increase your revenue there are things you can do by offering other services such as staining, crown molding etc. I always hired a handy man to go with me to the bigger jobs so I could offer all the services he was experienced in. People wanted a one stop shop and I was eager and very happy to accommodate them. This was a very important element to being able to expand my business and have more of a cash flow that would allow the expansion.

Q: What kind of equipment do you need to take on bigger jobs?

When that big client finally comes calling, it's important to be prepared. Sometimes, because more complicated equipment is expensive, it can take up to a year to get everything you need in order. If you've been cultivating a relationship with your paint store and have good credit, you can get credit from them to get that equipment, and pay it off monthly. When you do, make sure you are never late on a payment, because the store is very important when you want to upgrade your equipment and services.

One of the most profitable things you can get is a sprayer. A sprayer allows you to paint exteriors in a tenth of the time that you can with brushes or rollers. This is particularly helpful when you start doing commercial real estate. You can get the sprayer on credit, and it will immediately start paying for itself.

Another key piece of equipment for bigger jobs is a pressure cleaner. I would frequent places like going out of business sales that carried this type of machinery such as pressure cleaners and professional sprayers and would get them at reduced prices. I would rent lifts that were essential for jobs where I needed to paint a five plus story building.

Q: What do I do about licenses and insurance?

It's important to be licensed, not just so you can comply with the law, but so that you look credible to potential customers. Nobody wants to feel like they're being flim-flammed, and showing that the state has said you're qualified to do the work means a lot.

Licensing varies from state to state. Comply with your local licensing bureau on their licensing requirements.

You can go online to get the information regarding licenses and insurances or find someone who can help you.

Q: What opportunities do I have besides painting now that my business has grown?

Remember when we talked about how to use your paint work as a springboard into other opportunities? It gets even better when you have a bigger operation. I have had a lot of success buying houses for investment, and it's all thanks to my business. When you have workers on the ground, they are among the first to learn when a house is going up for sale. I will buy houses, use my crew to fix them up (because that's what they know how to do anyway), and either flip them or keep them for rental income.

Plus, in the painting business you develop a feel for the real estate market. Every market has its ups and downs, and having a company like mine puts you in a position to get in when the market is down, so you maximize your profits.

Chapter Three

HOW TO OUTSHINE
YOUR COMPETITION

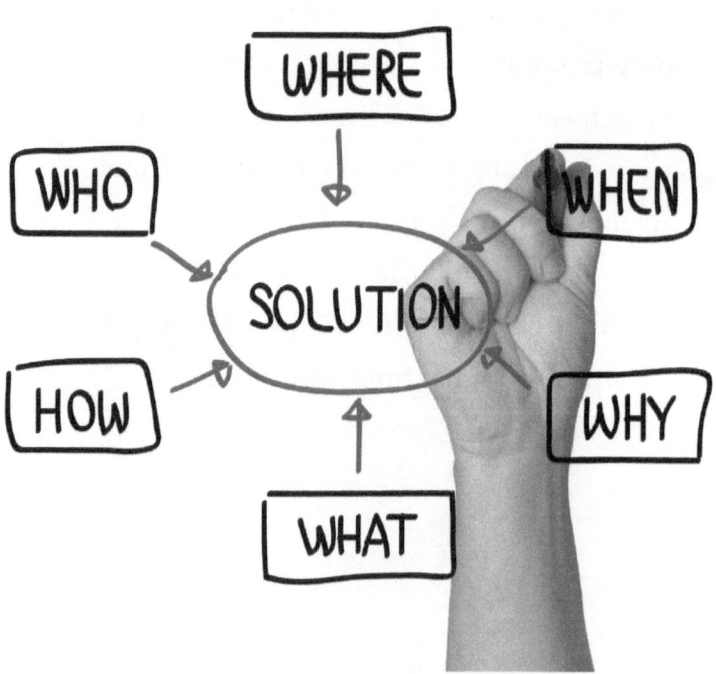

Here's a secret: it's not really about the painting. It's about the people, and how you treat them. It's about having the right attitude and being willing to go the extra mile. Whether you are just starting out or you're already underway, here are some important things to remember.

Lesson One: The most important thing is customer service:

There is great power in providing unexpected excellent customer service. When you go above and beyond what most of your competition is willing to do, you establish yourself as separate from the crowd, and you associate your brand with quality.

The first step to beating your competition, of course, is to know exactly what your competition is actually offering. You need to get to know the people you are outshining so you know exactly how to stand out in your customers' memory. Do your research and get as much information on other similar companies as you can. What are their prices? What services do they provide? What extras do they give, how do they reach and keep their customers and where do they operate from? Remember, when a potential customer is out there, he is looking at the same thing you are looking at when he goes out into the market.

It is important that your workers are professionally dressed, portray a good company image. Have them wear presentable shirts with your company logo and proper paint pants. Showing at the job on time, with courteous, friendly attitudes. Even if your price is very reasonable and competitive, and even if your work is excellent and you're careful to go that extra mile, you still might not stand out to your customer.

What you need to do is push it up a notch and give them the kind of service that truly amazes them, the little things that are so unexpected that a customer is completely taken by surprise by them. This unforgettable experience means, naturally, that you will not be forgotten in the crowd. It makes people feel loyal towards you, makes them say, "No thanks, I have already a great guy doing my painting" when they're approached by the competition.

It all begins with the first impression, and this moment is so fleeting and quick that you need to take full advantage of it - after all, you don't get a second chance to make that first impression. The first 3 seconds your client interacts with you and your workers, they've made up their mind about you. You may be tempted to skimp on uniforms or not worry too much about how professional the painters look, but projecting the right image is vitally important. Your client doesn't know a thing about you - they have to make a snap decision about you and your competence as professionals, and they'll do that with whatever information they see standing in front of them.

Lastly, the element of surprise will capture and keep the attention of your customer. If you create an experience that is memorable and different from anything your competition is providing, they'll be much, much more inclined to be pleased with your work and keep you in mind for further projects and referrals.

Don't stop just because you've won over a client. Your regular customers should be receiving lots of appreciation, communicating to them that you want them to keep coming back, that you are thankful for their business. A simple "thank you" can make the biggest difference when it comes to building customer loyalty.

Whatever you do, don't forget to regularly remind your longstanding customers that you appreciate them, and do not intend to take their support for granted. Send them emails expressing your gratitude or chat with them in person, but be sincere. Your client can at any time go to one of your competitors - you need to consistently give them reasons not to.

In fact, it's this skill of being able to really put yourself in your client's shoes that will make it much easier to provide outstanding service. Turn your perspective from making your own business work to figuring out how you can benefit *them*. What do they need? What do they see when they look at you and your staff? What do they want from your company and how can you give them even more than they hoped for?

Regularly go to sites and make sure that your staff is behaving professionally and appropriately. If it's a residential contract, you have to remember that when it comes to people's homes, you need to be extra careful that you are portraying respectful and considerate behavior. Are the staff having inappropriate conversations or smoking inside? Are they rude or disruptive? Remember, this may be the only part of your company that the client sees, so it's very important that your workers are doing their best.

I learned the power of customer service very early, in the simplest way. When I first started, I noticed that people seemed to like when I wore foot covers in their homes. These are simple little plastic foot covers to go over your shoes so that you don't make too much mess as you're going in and out. It's a little thing, but it communicates to them that I respect them and value their business. It doesn't cost much (the covers are actually reusable) but what it could potentially earn me in repeat business is well worth it. I noticed that I would always get good feedback about those covers, so I made a point to wear them as a matter of routine. Most people had never seen something like that before.

Think about it: if you're paying someone to improve the appearance of your house, what are you going to think of someone who just barges in and tracks mud all over everything? When you do something inconsiderate like this, and I've noticed that a lot of painters do, you're telling your customer that you're going to give them sloppy work. You're telling them you have so much business that you couldn't care less if they come back to you or not. Most likely you won't get hired, rehired or referred, end of story.

Dealing with Complaints

Of course, even if you've only been in the service industry for five minutes, you probably know that no matter what you do, you will get that one customer who will complain. Even if it seems that the complaint is unwarranted, and even if you've done your best to be accommodating, your only response to any customer complaint is to take it seriously and show your client that you intend to make things right. There is only one boss: the customer. You need to do whatever it takes to do to smooth any ruffled feathers and get back to being friends.

Very often, customers complain when they don't feel as though they or their business are being taken seriously. Ignore complaints of this kind at your own peril: if you don't take care of your customer, someone else will. In fact, being in business for a while, I've come to learn that it's often those customers that give you a really hard time that you have the most to learn from. Sometimes, although it's hard to admit, a customer can really shine a light on what you could be doing better.

Don't argue or get offended - take the opportunity to learn and grow from the experience. In many cases, a difficult client may turn out to be a loyal and repeat customer. So always demonstrate to them that you are not like your competition and if they are unhappy, you will bend over backwards to sort it out. Send a heartfelt letter of apology or better yet go in person to make things right. It may be temporarily uncomfortable to swallow your pride, and occasionally you may lose money if you've messed up and a client is angry, but it's nothing compared to your reputation, your sense of honor and your ability to follow through with what you promise as a superior service provider. I've always liked the saying: what you talk about, you bring about. Running my own business has taught me that no matter what happens in life, you need to be resilient, look for solutions and keep to your values. With a good attitude, you stand less chances of putting your client on the defensive and with the right mindset you can get to patching things up as quickly as possible. Your attitude shouldn't be to quibble over details - you know how irritating this can be if you're the client yourself - but rather, acknowledge and respect the complaint, and move on quickly to what you can do for them to patch things up.

Lesson Two: Be good to your workers

I was nervous, at first, hiring new people. It was a question of asking myself, every time I had a new worker, are they the right fit for this company? Are they going to do the job as well as I would - or better? Because I understood how much of the business rested on these little things, I had to be careful about who I chose. We were just a painting company, sure, but what made us a successful painting company was that we were so, so much more than just painting.

I know a lot of companies just hire someone and think that's the end of it. But I wanted to train my new people, make sure that they were accurate representatives of my company. There was no way I would let loose a new guy, no matter how skilled or experienced he was. If he was new in the company, either I or the foreman would have to spend some time with him, really making sure he knew how we did things.

It's good business to pay your workers well. I made sure that no matter what was happening with the company, their salaries were always paid on time. For those with more experience and better craftsmanship, I paid more, and in return they were loyal. I tried to get people with a range of skills so that I could use them when my clients needed something special done. We tried to diversify: if someone wanted a few extra odd jobs done while we painted, I liked being able to tell them that we could do it.

If your workers are unhappy, they're going to go out there and do bad work in your name. If your clients are unhappy, not only do you lose their business in the future, but you shut the door on every single referral they could have given you. If you have a poor relationship with the paint store, or you constantly get behind in paying them, you will lose their referrals too and will say goodbye to a hefty discount. Always take care of your foreman so he will be diligent about taking good care of things while you're away. The entire business works when each of these elements work together, and the way they work together is communication, good rapport and long term relationships.

Lesson Three: Think like an entrepreneur

Becoming an entrepreneur takes an adjustment in mindset. You can't wait passively for someone to explain things to you - you merely have to get out there and try things for yourself. Nobody will hold your hand, and if you're waiting for someone nice to come along and give you a big break, you may be waiting for a very long time. Here are some things that helped me keep in the right frame of mind:

Be passionate

It's easier to be uninspired when you work for someone else, when you work for yourself - you do just that, you work *for* yourself. Your passion for what you're doing will be the engine that drives everything forward. It will be the thing that gets you up in the morning, and the thing that helps you push through tight months and difficult clients. You'll need conviction in what you are doing.

For me, my conviction was that I wanted to do things on my own terms. I never wanted to work for other people, to hack away and build up their dreams for them. I wanted my own dreams. And the cost of that was not cheap: I had to be responsible and work hard. My passion, though, and my values held it all together. If I didn't care, I would have given up a long time ago. In a regular job, you answer to your boss. You have to do your thing because you're being paid. When you work for yourself, you answer to your own conscience. You have to find what makes you passionate.

More risk, more reward

Being someone else's employee is easy. You forfeit your own decision-making, and all the big risk falls on someone else's shoulders. But as an entrepreneur, you need to get comfortable taking that risk on your own shoulders.

You can't be too timid or afraid of making a leap of faith. It's true that the more you risk, the greater the chances for growth. I had to swallow my ego early on and just jump right in. If I failed, so what? I tried. I had to be OK with failing, I had to see failing as part of succeeding, to get comfortable with it, and to get out there and do new things. The person who can say, I don't know how to do this, is going to learn long before the person who's too afraid of looking like he doesn't know what he's doing.

Don't waste

In a big organization, when someone else is footing the bill, you might be tempted to be free and easy with the office stationery, to come into work a couple of minutes late each day or to pay just a little less attention to following up leads and caring for customers than you technically could have. After all, it doesn't really matter. But as an entrepreneur, this kind of inefficiency is your worst enemy. You need to keep your ears pricked for people who are frittering away revenue through sloppy work, inefficient quoting or wasting time.

Don't get too comfortable

Strive to reach your goals. But don't stop there. When you feel like you're meeting old challenges with ease, it's a sign that you need to challenge yourself more. For an entrepreneur, the work is never finished. You are never "done" with your business. There is always room to grow, opportunities that you can develop, connections you can make, and ways to streamline your work flow. Unless you're stretching yourself, reaching challenging new goals, broadening the business or learning new things, you're too comfortable. Is there anything you could be doing better?

Conclusion

I hope that in this short book, I've managed to convince you that if you really want it, working hard and building your own successful business is more than possible. After a taste of working in a corporate office environment, my opinion was settled: if you want work that is meaningful to you, if you want the excitement of making your own decisions and taking your own risks, and most importantly if you want the thrill of working hard to create something that you can take pride in, then I would recommend without any doubt that you consider entrepreneurship.

I had very little when I started, but I became very good at taking what I did have and using it to its fullest. At every step, I tried to grow, tried to push myself and tried to become better at what I offered. Through it all, the most important lesson that I learned was that businesses are about people. They're about getting out there and making connections, offering value, nurturing relationships. On an even more personal note, being my own boss has meant something a lot more profound to me than financial success or freedom. It has forced me to be a better person, to be kind, to be efficient and to never let my fear get the better of me.

Every day I would ask myself what was possible, and every day I pushed myself to achieve that. As a human being, I feel fulfilled in my ability to take nothing and turn it into something.

If you're stuck working for someone else, and think there's no way you can ever get out, then you are exactly the person I want to tell my story to. You can do it! The fear is an illusion. Working for someone else can be fulfilling, but it will never give you the sense of satisfaction and purpose that you can get from following your own path. I know that at the end of my life, I built something that was all my own. Your destiny is up to you. What will you build?

Footnote

In this book, I have shared my personal experiences in the painting industry, including the strategies that have been successful and the mistakes that I learned from. The strategies that I have outlined are only suggestions. Each business owner has their own method for achieving success. These are mine. My hope is that my suggestions and experience will be beneficial for anyone who reads this book.

GO AHEAD, PAINT YOURSELF TO YOUR AMERICAN DREAM!

Kurt Degen, Author

www.ingramcontent.com/pod-product-compliance
Lightning Source LLC
Chambersburg PA
CBHW031500210526
45463CB00003B/1011